I'M OKAY

By Courtney Corson

I don't like when Mommy leaves me.

Where is Mommy?

Mommy is cooking.

I am **sad**.

But I'm okay.

Where is Mommy?
Mommy is doing laundry.

I am **crying**.

But I'm okay.

Where is Mommy?

Mommy is taking a shower.

I am **frustrated**.

But I'm okay.

Where is Mommy?
Mommy is cleaning.

I am **angry**.

But I'm okay.

Where is Mommy?

Mommy is gardening.

I am **nervous**.

But I'm okay.

Where is Mommy?
Mommy is washing dishes.

I am **hesitant**.

But I'm okay.

Where is Mommy?

Mommy is fixing the light.

I am **curious**.

But I'm okay.

Mommy always comes back.
She snuggles and plays with me.

I am **happy**.

I'm okay!

Copyright 2023 Courtney Corson

All Rights Reserved

Written by Courtney Corson 2023

Illustrated by Federica Calloni 2023

www.ingramcontent.com/pod-product-compliance
Lightning Source LLC
Chambersburg PA
CBRC102011060526
44119CB00119B/363